DOWN UNDER PAR

DOWN UNDER PAR

by Charlie Earp
with Peter Murphy

Foreword by Greg Norman

Taylor Publishing Company
Dallas, Texas

Dedication

I dedicate this book to my mother, Kathleen;
To the memory of my late father, Edwin Charles;
Especially to my dear and devoted wife,
    Margaret, and my loving family;
To my mentor, Reg Want, and his family;
To the Royal Queensland Golf Club and
    its practice fairway (where all the work
    is done);
To all my trainees and pro shop 'assistants' over
    the years;
And to golfers the world over.

Let golf be an inspiration to achievement.

Illustrations by Cliff Sheldrake.

Originally published under the title *Charlie Earp Teaches You Golf* by Horwitz Grahame of Australia

Published by Taylor Publishing Company
            1550 West Mockingbird Lane
            Dallas, Texas 75235

Library of Congress Cataloging-in-Publication Data

Earp, Charlie.
    [Charlie Earp teaches you golf]
    Down under par / by Charlie Earp with Peter Murphy.
        p.   cm.
    "Originally published under title Charlie Earp teaches you golf by Horwitz Grahame of Australia." — T.p. verso.
        ISBN 0-87833-713-X : $9.95
        1. Golf. I. Murphy, Peter. II. Title.
    GV965.E27   1990
    796.352'3 — dc20

                                                    89-77052
                                                    CIP

Printed in the United States of America
10 9 8 7 6 5 4 3 2 1

FOREWORD

A ny great teacher has the ability to take a complex subject and divide it into the simplest components. Charlie Earp has that gift — his simple and basic ideas on how to play golf have made Charlie the best golf teacher in Australia, as evidenced by the knowledge and success of his pupils.

Charlie and I are the best of friends. We play golf together, we go fishing together, and he has even caddied for me in major championships, most memorably the 1984 US Open when we went to a play-off against Fuzzy Zoeller.

He is still my only teacher, even if sometimes that means talking by telephone from 10,000 miles away.

I worked two years for Charlie, beginning in 1975, as an assistant professional at Royal Queensland Golf Club. His advice and instruction started me on a successful path that has crisscrossed the globe.

For a while there, some members at Royal Queensland were content just to have me banned to a corner of the practice ground. I practised so much in those days, I was ripping a path of divots across the entire practice teeing area.

To achieve any success, you too must follow Charlie's teachings — and practice, practice.

Greg Norman

CONTENTS

INTRODUCTION: A Fulfilling Career 1

BIOGRAPHY: They Seek Him Here ... Seek Him There 5

NORMAN: A Different Kettle Of Fish 17

1 — Forget Those Mechanical Techniques 25

2 — Hands Must Work As A Team 27

3 — Quick Hands The Secret To Distance 39

4 — Focus On The Ball To Block Out Distractions 45

5 — Set-up Just Like Clockwork 49

6 — Develop Your Own Swing 57

7 — Fan Clubhead On The Backswing 65

8 — Turn Under The Nose 69

9 — Wrist Action Like Swatting A Fly 71

10 — Big Follow-through Adds Metres 75

11 — The Waggle Beats Cold Starts 77

12 — Consistency Comes From A Controlled Swing Pace . . 81

13 — The Art Of Drawing And Fading 85

14 — Will Putts Into The Hole 93

15 — Swing Stays The Same In Fairway Bunkers 105

16 — Don't Be Greedy In The Rough 109

17 — Confidence Can Cure The Yips 113

18 — The Psychology Of Teamwork 121

19 — Don't Rush Practice — It's A Learning Process . . . 123

20 — Hogan's Determination An Inspiration 125

A FULFILLING CAREER

WELCOME to my first book of golf instruction and, through reading and learning from it, you will share with me one of the loves of my life — a marvellously engrossing sport intended for enjoyment, relaxation and friendship. As you read of my history, you will see how I came almost accidentally into this game that I previously knew nothing about.

I often marvel at how lucky I have been to be able to spend so many years doing something that I find so fulfilling. The manifestation of this over the years is seen in following the progress of youngsters I have tutored. I have witnessed improvement in their games as they mature, with many achieving single figures in their mid-teens.

Adjustments to the swing are necessary as the player grows taller and stronger until, at maturity, he or she should have a well-grooved action. From that stage only practice and mental discipline will improve scoring.

For those people now into mature age, don't despair. If you are thinking of taking up golf, there is nothing to stop you from developing your golf muscles through practice and play and fashioning a swing to suit your physical make-up.

I have written this book primarily as a guide for the beginner and, to this end, the text is brief and to the point. There is no maze of technical detail, embellishment or superfluous matter to clutter the mind. I don't do that on

Making an adjustment to the backswing of Queensland junior representative, 17-year-old Trudi Jeffrey.

the practice tee with my pupils and I have no intention of doing that here. The objective of golf is to hit a ball and the best way to achieve that is to keep everything simple — from instruction through to the swing. The basics I teach are in the simplicity of the swing and by learning correctly from the start the whole procedure is uncomplicated.

Fear is the main reason why many beginners duff shots or have air swings. Through this book I will endeavour to dispel any fear about striking the ball and show you how easy it can be. And it will be easy if you simply follow my advice, which is the same advice I give to all my pupils, from Greg Norman down. Get it right the first time and then it will simply be a case of practising in order to be able to play to the best of your ability. Practice ... now there's a word that goes hand in glove (pardon the pun) with golf. You can't expect to achieve any standard of success unless you practice. That applies to all bat and ball games.

The text provides basic instruction and requires careful study if you are to attain a fundamentally sound swing. And because it is written instruction, you will need to have a golf club with you to put into practice what you read in the step-by-step lessons with their photographic and artwork illustrations. Don't wait until you get onto a golf course to give it a go — that's not the place to practise. If you try to take a multitude of instruction onto a course, you'll be a failure.

If you get the opportunity to play with good golfers, do so. It will be a lesson in itself, studying their swing actions and how they hit the ball. With few exceptions, the outstanding players have uncomplicated and seemingly effortless swings and the ability to concentrate 100 per cent on every shot. You can see it in their eyes how well they concentrate, focusing intensely on the ball and, by doing so, shutting themselves off from any distractions.

Golf is a game of patient learning, from the time your game is 'born' to the time you're ready to meet the 'Ultimate Handicapper'.

Here's a triple salute to the Australian Flying Doctors with three of Greg Norman's famous Akubra hats. The hats, worn by Greg during his 1986–1987 Australian circuit campaign, were donated to a Rotary charity auction to help raise funds for the aerial medical service. The Akubras were part of my luggage during my world trip in 1987 and were autographed by Greg at his Orlando home in Florida before heading off to Scotland for the British Open. Photo: courtesy of the *Daily Sun* and *Sunday Sun* newspapers, Brisbane.

'THEY SEEK HIM HERE ... SEEK HIM THERE'

'T HE family is very proud of Charlie. Right from when he started he's given up his weekends for golf... he likes to help the young players.' These are the words of 73-year-old Kathleen Monica Earp, mother of one of the world's greatest coaches in one of the world's most exacting sports.

Known in Australia as the 'guru of coaches', Charlie Earp has produced a string of champions, both amateur and professional, from his Royal Queensland Golf Club pro shop near the banks of the Brisbane River. And the best of the crop is Greg Norman, who, as a trainee, enthused his boss with his boasting that he was 'gunna be the best player in the world'.

The remarkable achievements of Norman on the international tour have brought justifiable fame to his mentor, so much so that Earp's telephone rings constantly and opening bundles of mail is a never-ending job for his wife and pro shop 'secretary', Margaret. There are requests by the hundred each month, from throughout Australia and overseas, asking for lessons with the skilful tutor. They come from the United States, Canada, England, South Africa and, closer to home, from New Zealand and New Guinea.

A happy and proud moment for me as I receive my Advance Australia Award in 1986 for services to golf from Queensland's Governor, Sir Walter Campbell.

Numbered among his pupils have been some big names of stage and screen — Agent 007 himself, James Bond, who turned up as actor Sean Connery, American singers Johnny Mathis and Charlie Pride and English comedian Eric Sykes. Then there are requests almost every month from far and wide from parents wanting their sons to be apprenticed to Earp. As much as he would like to assist, a courteous 'unable to oblige' is sent by return mail.

For Charlie Earp, golf is his life's work — the love of his life. He has poured his heart and soul into the game since he began his traineeship in 1953, at the age of 15, with former Queensland Open champion Reg Want at Coolangatta-Tweed Heads Club on the southern tip of the Gold Coast.

Five years later on December 1, a lean, 5 ft 7 in (170 cm), unknown 19-year-old — who looked as though he couldn't hit a ball out of his shadow — walked undauntedly through the gates of the illustrious Royal Queensland Golf Club to take up an appointment as club professional.

Royal Queensland initially sought former assistant Want himself for the job — a player with a valued reputation and a tournament record to back it up. Want was happy where he was, but he was quick to put in a good word for his protégé who, at the time, was just settling in as the new club pro at Lismore in northern New South Wales. Young Charlie accepted the advice of his former boss for the Royal Queensland position ... a decision he has never regretted and certainly one which, had he by-passed, would not have led to his association with Greg Norman, 16 years later.

Earp had precious little time to try to make a name for himself as a tournament player. It was business first, and that left almost no time for practice. He won some trainee matches, a

Beggin' your pardon, Ma'am, but we just borrowed some of your sheep's feed bins to use as props so that we could add a touch of royal flavour to our photograph. That's me, Charles (now isn't that a regal name) and my Scottish friend Anne Bell (and that has a royal ring to it as well) outside her property near Muirfield in 1987 when I was in Scotland for the British Open. Anne and husband Alistair breed goats for the cashmere industry and when this big red carrier arrived to cart them north for sale, the Queen Mother's sheep were on board. So, not one to miss an opportunity, I grabbed Anne for a family album snapshot with Her Majesty's sheep feed bins. The sheep were too shy to emerge from the truck, but the family dog Nell was keen to get into the act. My wife Margaret and I met the Bells during our 1980 British Open tour. We stayed at their property a short while and became friends.

couple of pro-ams and a 36-holer. But from the time of his appointment at Royal Queensland, he focused his attention on teaching and later on became heavily involved in administrative work and promotion of the game.

* * *

There wasn't much of Charles Howarth Earp when he took his first gasp of air at St Margaret's Private Hospital, Murwillumbah, in the Tweed district of northern New South Wales on June 26, 1938. He weighed 6½ lb (2.95 kg) — and there still isn't much of him today; he weighs 9 st 3 lb (58.5 kg) wringing wet. The first of five children born to Edwin Charles (died 1970) and Kathleen Monica Earp, little 'Chilla' had a lot of get up and go when he played around his parents' farming properties in the Murwillumbah district village of Crystal Creek and later at Closeburn on the north-western outskirts of Brisbane. He loved riding the farm horses and galloped them around in fearless fashion. Such was his ability in the saddle that he was offered an apprenticeship as a jockey. But his parents said 'no', fearing for the safety of their son.

Earp also could have made a name for himself as a rugby league footballer. While attending Coolangatta State School on the southern end of the Gold Coast, after the family moved to the area when Charlie was nine, he displayed outstanding footballing skills and was appointed captain of the school's senior team. Another outstanding member of that team was a kid called Barry Muir, who went on to represent Australia in Test matches. Young Charlie was under consideration for a State age representative spot, but he was ruled ineligible because of an age restriction as a result of his birthday falling mid-year.

Bruce Crampton, the first Australian to win $1 million from golf, is one of the many great players whom I have used in my swing studies.

Then, at the age of 15, along came the apprenticeship offer from Coolangatta-Tweed Heads pro Reg Want and Charlie's dedication to the Royal and Ancient game began from day one. Earp, thus, began his golfing career as a professional, never having hit one golf ball as an amateur. No member of the Earp family had ever had anything to do with golf up till then and, coincidentally, it was at this age that Charlie's star pupil, Greg Norman, took up the game.

As for recreation, these days Charlie enjoys a spot of fishing, when he can afford the time away from Royal Queensland and other commitments. He sometimes sets sail for Fraser Island off the southern Queensland coast with fellow pros or family friends and, as the story goes, there are more tinnies of the amber brew opened than fish caught.

*   *   *

Earp's skills as a teacher were derived from studying the swings of some of the world's greatest players while they practised and competed in tournaments at home and abroad. He would stand for long periods just watching and absorbing the techniques of players like Arnold Palmer, Norman von Nida, Gary Player, Peter Thomson, Kel Nagle, Julius Boros, Bruce Crampton, Ossie Pickworth, Billy Dunk ... the list goes on. And probably to his detriment as a player, Earp sometimes would mimic the swings of some of the greats, imagining he was in their shoes — Palmer one day, Player the next. However, he later found that this was to work to his advantage as a tutor. All the knowledge he had stored from watching the champions practise and play he was able to pass on to his pupils.

Technique is not of paramount importance when Earp takes beginners and average

The 'old' Royal Queensland Golf Clubhouse, with the pro shop at left, where Greg Norman began his professional career and was regarded as a 'menace' on the practice tee because of the thousands of divots he tore out of the ground. He was barred from the area at one stage.

players for lessons. It's the simplicity of the
golf swing. One of his biggest attributes is that
he 'speaks their language'. He doesn't create
confusion in their minds with too much
technical talk. Earp freely admits that there
have been occasions when he 'couldn't get
through' to some people. When this happens
he suggests they might do better seeing
another pro, whom he recommends.

Being a good listener while doing his time
also held Earp in good stead for his coaching
career. Apart from his peers, there were
several amateurs who helped him to
understand the game better.

* * *

The esteem in which Earp is held by his
colleagues was clearly demonstrated in 1963
when, as a mature 24-year-old, he was elected
president of the Queensland PGA. Along with
this responsibility he won a seat on the
executive of the Australian PGA and was a
member of the national trainee committee. In
recognition of his services he was awarded life
membership in 1978.

In 1982 he gained the seal of approval from
the Queensland Golf Union to coach the State
senior and junior amateur teams. And since
the rise of Greg Norman to golfing fame, more
and more youngsters throughout the State
have been doing their darnedest to bring their
handicaps down to single figures in the hope
of winning a place in one of Earp's training
squads.

Those who succeed quickly discover that the
master coach is also a master of a different
kind — a task master. He won't take any
nonsense from his young pupils and those
who fail to follow his instructions may well find
themselves looking for another tutor. Yet, Earp
will go beyond the call of duty if he spots any

Fortune favours the brave . . . and that's how I viewed it when I strode barefoot into the lake on the par four 12th at Florida's Bay Hill course in Orlando during a practice round with Greg Norman in 1985. My drive finished in this water hazard, but with a little touch of magic — and with the help of a six iron — I extricated the ball onto the green and, do you mind, only 8ft from the flag.

of his talented kids in need of extra attention, giving them a 'free' private lesson or two outside the scheduled weekend squad sessions. He also is co-coach with Robbie Taylor, of Brisbane's Pacific Club, in the School of Excellence, a Queensland Golf Union funded operation which teaches the Royal and Ancient game weekly to selected high school students in the metropolitan area.

All this on top of the constant flow of club coaching commitments for Royal Queensland members and an endless queue of visitors who 'seek him here ... seek him there' for a lesson. It's enough to send any man grey with worry.

Yet, it doesn't end there.

Earp's latest challenge, and probably the most demanding of his career, has been put before him at the request of his prize pupil, the one they call The Great White Shark. Norman's eagerness to 'put something back into golf' in his home State of Queensland has led to the establishment of the Greg Norman Junior Golf Foundation. Earp and long-serving Queensland Golf Union secretary Bill Kennedy are involved in administering the foundation, expected to cost $500,000 in this its first year of operation. The purpose of the foundation is to encourage and foster junior golf throughout the State, particularly in country areas.

Kennedy has known Earp for 26 years and describes him as 'one of nature's gentlemen … a fellow whose word is his bond and if he promises to do something, I've never known him yet to let anybody down. He's the busiest professional in Queensland and probably the busiest in Australia. You'd go a long way to find a more dedicated fellow in the game. If he charged for everything he does, he'd be a millionaire.'

A millionaire! That's a real prospect for Earp. He has been guaranteed such earnings if he pulls up roots and heads off to America to set up shop. He's thought about it, and that's as far as it's gone.

Maybe he might allow himself a year in the US to advance his knowledge of the game and the latest teaching methods. But Charlie Earp is as 'true blue' as kangaroos, cockatoos and Sunday arvo barbecues with the missus, his mates and the billy lids. What more could a man ask for?

PETER MURPHY

Overseeing Norman at work in the bullring at The Shark's home course in Orlando, Florida. A news media photographer made a close inspection to get some tips.

NORMAN: A DIFFERENT KETTLE OF FISH

GREG Norman is the greatest hitter of a golf ball who has ever been born ... and I'm not saying that because I am his coach. He may not be the best scorer, but nobody has been born yet who can hit the ball like Greg Norman. Jack Nicklaus can't hit the ball like Greg. Nicklaus has his own way of hitting the golf ball ... so did Ben Hogan and all the great players.

Greg is a different kettle of fish when it comes to long, consistent hitting of woods and irons. And when his short game is honed to an even higher standard, he could go on to be the greatest scorer of all time. Maybe some people will disagree and say that Hogan was better. I think that Hogan was the straightest and most consistent hitter ever, but he wasn't as long as Greg, or as strong.

Greg is working on being better than Hogan for consistency in accuracy. I know that his ambitions are high and he is faced with an enormous hurdle when you consider the career feats of Hogan, Jack Nicklaus, Tom Watson, Sam Snead and others, but Greg has

A younger Greg Norman, hard at work practising at Royal Queensland.

the ability to become the greatest golfer the world has ever seen. He practises for hours playing difficult shots from off the fairway, out of trees, the rough, quick elevation shots, low ones under branches. This is so that when he does stray with a drive he's able to recover without, hopefully, dropping a shot.

He is now working on getting the ball on the fairway with every drive and on hitting the green with every approach shot, like Hogan did. Hogan was such a great player that in his 1953 British Open win at Carnoustie he paced out the course and ascertained where he needed to hit the ball from the tee and where he needed to put the ball short of the flag so he didn't leave a downhill putt. He put shots where he wanted them for uphill putts and the chances of knocking in birdies. That's the sort of thing that makes champions.

And that's what Greg wants to be able to do. He is now condensing himself into that kind of player ... to be able to do those sorts of things instead of just attacking the top of the flag. You can only become that good through playing in major tournaments and playing with the champions and learning about how good they are and were.

I believe that Greg Norman has the ability and confidence to carry him to victory in all four major championships. I am not going to say that he would beat the amazing record of Nicklaus, but I know in his (Norman's) own heart that he wants to surpass the feats of the Golden Bear.

Greg's best golfing years are ahead of him. Look at Nicklaus winning the 1986 US Masters at the age of 46. It was a fantastic effort shooting that great final round of 65, with a back nine of 30 that included five birdies and an eagle. It was one of the greatest nine-hole scores that Nicklaus had ever shot.

I would have loved to have seen Greg win

19

the Masters, but I got a fantastic thrill seeing Nicklaus succeed at his age.

I don't think I should be taking so much credit for Greg Norman, or for what he has achieved. I was just a lucky guy to get mixed up with him — and we clicked. Our serious association began in 1973 when he was showing great promise at the age of 17. He would come to Royal Queensland to practise and he was such a dedicated young player that I took a great interest in him. In between lessons I could see him in the background and, if he was having problems, I would go and have a look at him to advise him. After practising any changes, he would come back to me and say: 'Hey, have I got it right now?'

He was so meticulous and he practised for so long that in some areas we had to bar him because he dug up the practice fairways so much.

When he started doing his time with me early in 1975, we didn't work on long shots to any great degree, it was mainly short stuff — half shots and learning to play low shots into the breeze. I remember saying to him one time: 'You are going to learn to hit the ball lower because, if you're talking about going to England and if you hit the ball as high there, especially around London, it is going to end up in Paris. The wind will just take it straight across the English Channel.'

He didn't believe me at first, saying he believed the wind in England should not greatly affect the high ball. His game at that stage was very high because he structured it on the modern American method. I told him he would need to learn how to play the punch shot — to get the ball down quail-high. I showed him how to play the ball low with a fade and a draw. Instead of taking a six iron, you take a five or four iron and play it in real low.

He still didn't think it was right, saying: 'This isn't the way I read golf.' That's because he had the American idea of playing golf — hitting the ball high to get as much carry as possible.

When Scottish pro, Tom McNaughton, arrived on the practice fairway, I called him over and, in Greg's presence, asked him: 'Thomas, how do you have to play the ball at St Andrew's or Muirfield or any of those coastal courses in Scotland and England?'

Tom answered in his Scottish brogue: 'Yee gotta be keepin' the bluudy thing as low as yee possibly can.'

Greg looked at me and said: 'All right, I believe you, show me again.'

Tom and I worked with him for a little while then Greg spent a day and a half just practising that punch shot.

About 11 a.m. on the second day, he walked into the pro shop and said: 'I've got it. Come and have a look at it.'

So we went back out to the bullring together and he could play this shot — he could do whatever he wanted with it. He could make the ball talk!

He worked hard to finesse the shot and, in doing so, got away from the stereotype of golf that he had read about in books from America. He thought that was how you played golf. He didn't realise how well Nicklaus, Snead, Hogan, Trevino, Hagen and the top-line players could manoeuvre the ball. Greg has used the punch shot many times on tour and it has made a lot of money for him. It gave him control when he was under a bit of pressure.

I also had to change his grip. It was too palmy. At one stage he came to me for help because he was hitting the ball left and right, saying: 'I would like to play with a fade but every now and then I get a drag.' I told him the problem was his grip, having too much of the

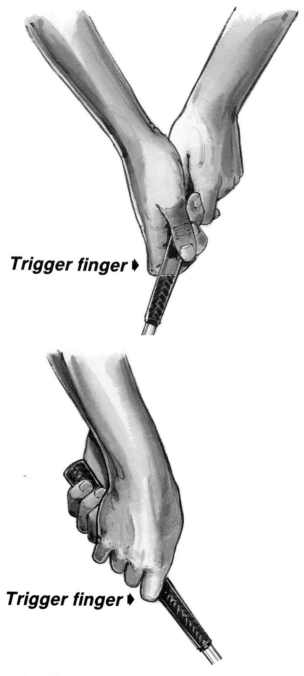

Trigger finger ▸

Trigger finger ▸

Greater control and distance results from correct use of the forefinger of the bottom hand, known as the trigger finger. Place the grip across the middle knuckle of the forefinger so that it acts as a hook. I showed this method to Greg Norman when he was my trainee, and look what happened to him.

club in the palm of his right hand. I told him he had to get the club in the trigger point of his forefinger to allow him to use the right hand to full capacity.

He said: 'Show me where to put it?' And when I did, he looked me right in the eye and said: 'Nobody plays with a grip like that!'

I answered: 'Well, Harry Vardon did, and Snead and Hogan, and Nicklaus and Palmer ... Thomson, Nagle and Henry Cotton did.'

Greg just couldn't believe it.

About 18 months later, after having been successful in a few tournaments, he was conducting a clinic for businessmen at Royal Queensland and he said to them: 'If you want to hit the ball straighter and stronger, you will need to take the club in the bottom hand like this (demonstrating) and you can hit the ball as hard as you like with the right hand. And if you don't believe me, go and ask that little .... under the tree over there.' He was pointing to me sitting nearby under a Moreton Bay fig.

Talking about businessmen, Greg has been, at times, a difficult man to manage. He has a mind of his own, as many people are aware.

Nevertheless, he has always been willing to listen to the right advice, much of which has come from his father Merv and mother Toini, of whom he speaks very highly. He loves them very much.

Three other people who have been highly influential in the life of Greg Norman, both with business management and personally, are Australia's former Federal Minister for Defence, Sir James Killen, a close friend Cyril King and the former president and captain of Royal Queensland Club, Doug Cranstoun. Greg has always been prepared to listen to their words of wisdom.

Greg and I have had a pretty good rapport since we first linked up, but there have been some little disagreements. I recall when he was assistant pro with me and he was talking then about wanting to be the world's No. 1 golfer. 'I'm going to be the best player in the world,' he would say.

We had a few arguments about that and once I told him rather sternly: 'There are two bloody brick walls out the front there (indicating the entrance gates to the club). If you don't like what you've got to do here, buddy, just walk through there and don't bother coming back!' He soon got the message that, although he had high ambitions, there was work to be done in the meantime, both in the shop and on the practice fairway.

I can recall his first win in the Martini International in 1977. I wrote him a letter and congratulated him and reminded him that it doesn't matter where you come from, when you are on tour you represent your club, your State, your country and you represent the game of golf ... 'make sure you are a great ambassador in all these throughout your life'.

I take interest in helping people to play golf; to make them proud of their club, of their zone, of their State and of Australia. I hope that what Greg Norman has done in an ambassadorial role for this country rubs off onto other sports' representatives of Australia. I am not just saying that because I'm a golfer and Greg is a golfer, but because of what he has done for Australian sport.

1
FORGET THOSE MECHANICAL TECHNIQUES

BECAUSE of the intricacies of golf, almost all of us have suffered mental hang-ups about our games at some time or another. It could have been the grip, the set-up, backswing, wondering if you're swaying or lunging at shots, a flying elbow or looking up before you have hit the ball. Or maybe it was one of those two perennial bogies which afflict most average golfers — the out-of-bounds slice or the duck-hook.

Even experienced professionals have been plagued by curly psychological problems affecting some aspect of their game. Some have never been able to shake them off, and this can be soul destroying.

One tip I can give you in trying to overcome these constant mental menaces is to practise and persevere in finding ways to conquer them.

Forget those mechanical techniques and get back to what the game of golf is all about: co-ordination and timing. Make it as simple as you can.

The biggest fear with beginners is the thought of missing the ball. Some have the fear of God in them about having an air swing. Why? I don't know. Nobody is going to punish them if they have an airy. They only punish themselves worrying about it. So, when I take beginners for a lesson, I tell them they are here to hit the golf ball but it is no crime if they miss it. Telling them this generally puts them at ease and helps eliminate the fear of missing a shot or two.

I also tell my students that I had to start from scratch, too, and somebody had to help me overcome many of the fears they experience as beginners. I had an inferiority complex. I didn't want to go on the golf course because I thought I would be a nuisance to the people I played with; I would hold up play; I wasn't sure of the rules; some experienced players might give me a hard time! So, I tell my students that if they are having problems and feel they are holding up play, they should pick up their ball and resume play at the next hole.

It generally takes 20 to 30 minutes of the first lesson to get beginners to hit the ball reasonably well. And that's the whole object of the game — to hit the ball. And the moment I have got them to elevate the ball off the ground, that is when they have proven something very important to themselves — that they can hit the ball into the air.

From there on it is just a matter of helping them work on their swings and develop the muscles they need to hit the ball. While playing golf, you are getting every muscle in your body functioning and you are using your brain to calculate shots.

Most men and women play the game simply because they want exercise, both physical and mental, and that's a healthy attitude to have.

2
HANDS MUST WORK AS A TEAM

A GOOD grip makes for a good swing. And it is important that you have a grip that suits the size of your hands. It may be the overlapping grip, the interlocking or the two-handed (baseball) grip. If you have big hands with long fingers, use the overlapping grip; short and stubby fingers are more suited to the interlocking method used by Nicklaus; or the two-handed style (where the thumb of the top hand is wrapped around the grip) could be more to your liking.

In all cases, the club is set in the hands the same way ... through the index finger of the top hand, across and under the palm pad and linking with the fingers of the bottom hand (see illustrations p. 30). Never grip the club too tightly. Just keep it firm enough to maintain control on the backswing and then, when entering the hitting zone, your brain will automatically tell you to grip the club tightly at impact — the same as in any other bat and ball game. If you hold the club like a vice, you will not release correctly on the shot. When under pressure or pumped up, it is essential

not to grip too strongly. This could cause a blocked shot or a hook.

A common fault with learners is that they tend to have the top hand (left for the right-hander) set too weak and the bottom hand too strong. That means that the back of the top hand is turned towards the ground and the palm of the bottom hand is facing the sky (turned too far under the shaft). You end up with one hand fighting against the other. The hands must work as a team for the swing to function correctly. There must be a uniting of the hands, a coupling together. Once that is done, the left hand (for the right-hander) becomes your guiding hand and the right hand is your driving force in hitting the ball.

Early this year one of Australia's finest international players, Peter Senior, came to me knowing he had something amiss with his grip but he was becoming frustrated in trying to pinpoint the fault. He said he felt he was losing control on his shots. I had known for some 18 months that his grip wasn't the best, but because he was 'working' with other people, I did not wish to interfere. After I saw him playing the 1987 British Open, I said to one of my associates: 'I'd love to have a crack at Peter Senior's grip.'

Well, he telephoned me in March and asked if I could help sort out the problem and, after watching him hit some balls, I noticed he was butterflying with his right hand (i.e. as he was preparing to hit the ball he was regripping with his right hand two or three times and gradually turning it clockwise under the shaft). Consequently, when he commenced his backswing, his right hand was out of position. His thumb was over the top of the shaft instead of being along the inside and he was gripping the club in the top knuckle of his right index finger instead of through the middle knuckle (the trigger point). This was

TOP HAND GRIP

LEFT: Lay the grip across the forefinger with the thumb placed short (not extended) over the top and the end of the grip tucked under the palm's lower muscle pad.

RIGHT: Close the fingers, putting pressure on the grip to hold it under the muscle pad. The pressure should only be firm enough to maintain control.

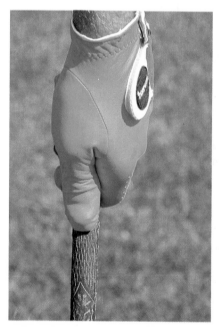

LEFT: Looking down at your hand you should see only the first two knuckles, and the V formed by the thumb and forefinger should point towards the opposite sides of your face. Turn to page 32 for bottom hand grip.

causing him to hook and block out shots under pressure and, as he said, he was not in control.

The message here is: Once you are correctly set up to play a shot, don't alter your grip.

After I corrected Peter's grip, he said it felt uncomfortable. I assured him it would work, so he set about hitting some 6000 balls during the next four or five days to try to become accustomed to that reset right hand. Even after having hit all those practice balls, he still said the 'new' hand position felt uncomfortable. However, the results of the adjustment were clearly evident as he was grouping his shots much better, narrowing his target radius by some 15 metres. Peter now has a grip that will work under pressure. He'll be in control.

Most good players, both amateur and professional, have not really refined their grips to where they should be — into the category of being able to narrow their margin of error.

Ossie Moore is another example. As a member of my Queensland amateur team in 1981, I noticed his grip was too palmy. He also held the club too high in his right index finger. When I adjusted Ossie's grip to the trigger finger position he didn't like the way it felt, saying it was very uncomfortable — as they all say.

I told him: 'Stick with it, it'll work.'

That year he went on to win the Australian Amateur Championship and later turned pro to become a player of distinction.

A similar story can be told about another Queenslander under my care, Corinne Dibnah, who did herself and her country proud in July by becoming the first Australian to win the women's British Open. Corinne has been a leading money winner on the European pro tour for the past three years and has the potential to become one of the world's best

BOTTOM HAND GRIP

LEFT: The grip is held from the trigger point (middle knuckle) of the forefinger across the fingers (not in the palm).

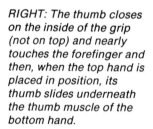

RIGHT: The thumb closes on the inside of the grip (not on top) and nearly touches the forefinger and then, when the top hand is placed in position, its thumb slides underneath the thumb muscle of the bottom hand.

LEFT: There is no gap between the thumb and forefinger when the grip is closed and the V points to the middle or right side of the face (if right-handed).

FULL GRIP

Both V's point in the same direction when the hands are closed together. It is important that the hands work as a team.

players. I also adjusted her right-hand grip in 1981, showing her the correct use of the trigger finger, and that same year she too captured the Australian amateur crown, as a junior.

Ask any qualified PGA teaching professional about the importance of the grip. He or she will tell you that it is the key factor to attaining a good swing. If the grip is faulty, no other element of the swing will function correctly — the hands and arms, the shoulders, legs or footwork. You can't bake a cake if you don't have the right ingredients.

POPULAR GRIP TYPES

This is the overlapping or Vardon grip, used by the majority of golfers throughout the world. The little finger of the bottom hand lays across the index finger of the top hand ... you can either place it on top or let it slide between the forefinger and the middle finger of the top hand. This overlapping method reduces pressure in the middle of the grip where it is not so important. The most important pressure areas are the top three fingers, the bottom three fingers and the inside of the bottom thumb.

The less common interlocking grip, suitable for players with short or stubby fingers or fat hands. Interlock the little finger of the bottom hand with the forefinger of the top hand which, again, minimises pressure in the middle of the grip.

HAND POSITION AT TOP OF BACKSWING

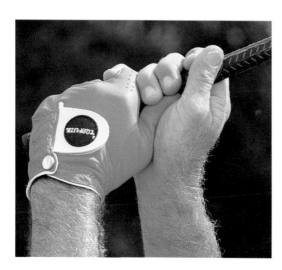

These pictures clearly indicate an ideal position once you have completed your backswing. Keep the left wrist firm and straight with the right or bottom hand under the grip.

HERE'S ONE WAY OF RUINING A SHOT...

These pictures show the result of over-swinging where the wrists are cupped or cocked too much, causing a cross-over effect which impedes pivot and invariably leads to slicing.

... AND HERE'S ANOTHER WAY TO 'KILL' IT.

More illustrations of an out-of-control position, with the right or bottom hand too far under the club and a bent top wrist which causes the clubface to close and face the sky. This tends to give a casting feeling from the top of the swing where the wrists uncock too early and will cause a blocked-out shot or a snap hook.

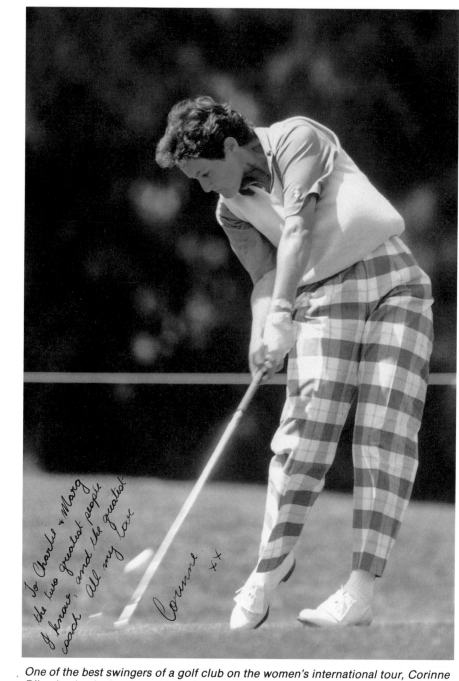

To Charlie + Marg
the two greatest people
I know, and the greatest
coach. All my love

Corinne
x x

One of the best swingers of a golf club on the women's international tour, Corinne Dibnah, clearly demonstrating here the trigger finger action with her right hand. A lot of hard work paid off for Corinne when she captured the 1988 Women's British Open, becoming the first Australian to do so. There's more big victories ahead for this outstanding golfing talent from Queensland.

3
QUICK HANDS THE SECRET TO DISTANCE

I ACHIEVE great results by getting my pupils to start with half a backswing. Apart from the grip and a parallel set-up, the most important thing beginners need to learn is how to hit the ball and make it rise in the air. Once they have proved they can do that, the next step is to practise to allow the muscles to become attuned to the swing.

The reason many golfers have difficulty in correctly hitting a ball is because they are unconsciously trying to 'lift' it in the air by scooping the shot with too much stiff-arm action or lunging.

Golf is a game of opposites: If you want the ball to rise, you hit down on it; if you want the ball to go left, you aim right; and vice versa.

Try to develop a feeling that you are going to hit the ball first then squeeze it through the ground; or feel that you are going to hit the ball at the horizon; or maybe feel that you are going to send the clubhead through low after the ball. Whatever the case, let the lofts on the clubfaces of all clubs in your bag do the job

Uncocking your wrists at the right time in the release zone can be likened to hammering a nail into a wall at knee level. If you hit too early or too late, you will miss the nailhead.

they are designed to do — make the ball rise. Elevation of the ball should not be a consideration in shotmaking.

Once you have become an accomplished player, by being able to swing with confidence without a thought of a mishit, you can then start giving the ball a bit of a 'ride'. By that I mean you can start hitting the ball hard, wherever the occasion warrants it for the purpose of gaining more distance.

It is a tremendous advantage over other competitors if you can get the ball out a long way. Hitting a golf ball a good distance has little to do with physical strength. The secret is in the hands. The ball will go nowhere by lunging or heaving your body at it or just stiff-arming the shot. You end up with all twist and no hit. Hand speed generates clubhead speed and the more of the latter you can produce the farther the ball will go. It all happens between the back knee and the front knee at the bottom of your swing arc. That's the crucial area where you release or uncock your wrists into the shot. It comes back to co-ordination and timing and certainly not a case of throwing your body at the ball. It doesn't matter how big and powerful a player may be, if he can't release his hands he can't get distance on the ball.

The longest hitters in golf, like Greg Norman, Seve Ballesteros, Fred Couples and Ian Woosnam, have the fastest hands through the release area. They uncock their wrists as late as possible and their hands move lightning fast, whipping the clubhead through the ball and giving it an almighty belt with the right hand. If you have seen these great hitters in action, you will have noticed that their balance is superb and fluent throughout their swing even though they are going for as much distance as possible. They know that the secret to distance is having quick hands ...

keeping their hands ahead of the ball as long as possible before powering through the shot, with their right hand being the dominant force.

Contrary to one school of thought, it is not the left hand (for the right-hander) which produces the hitting power. The left hand is your guiding instrument once you commence your downswing.

A method of learning how to hit the ball correctly with your hands is to stand with your feet together and practise hitting balls with only a three-quarter backswing. This will give you an appreciation of having to whip the clubhead through the shot with a late

Hit the ball with a descending blow to make it rise. Elevation of the ball should not be a consideration in shotmaking as the lofts on clubfaces are designed to do just that.

Better contact can result from a feeling that you are going to hit the ball first then squeeze it through the ground.

uncocking of the wrists in order to hit the ball a fair distance. Uncocking your wrists at the right time in the release zone can be likened to hammering a nail into a wall at about knee level. If you hit too early or too late, you are going to miss the nailhead.

For some beginners, it may take a couple of months before they can get their swings 'in the groove', with others it could be longer. Practice will pay off.

Looking at the ball intensely helps shut out distractions. Maintain your focus on the ball until you see it being struck by the clubhead.

4

FOCUS ON THE BALL TO BLOCK OUT DISTRACTIONS

A LOT of golfers, even some of the better players, forget to really look at the ball on impact. There are many pros who make this mistake. They are too busy worrying if their swing is right or if some aspect of their set-up is okay. They should be more intent on hitting the ball — and the back of the ball at that.

Do as the top players do: be intent on seeing the ball being struck by the clubhead. Just watch how intensely all the champions like Nicklaus, Norman and Ballesteros look 'hard' at the ball. This helps with concentration because by focusing your mind on hitting the ball it tends to shut out any noises or distractions around you.

Business people duff shots sometimes because they are thinking about making telephone calls or whether they have forgotten to do something at the office.

David Graham, a good example of a player who goes through a planned routine before playing a shot.

Distracting thoughts will not enter your mind if you are intent on hitting the ball.

And don't worry about keeping your head down either. That's a load of bunkum. A lot of people concentrate too much on keeping their heads down instead of looking at the ball. If you look at the ball your head will stay down. That's logic.

Concentration itself can sometimes be overdone and adversely affect shot preparation and shotmaking. Some players go out for a game saying to themselves: `I've got to concentrate ... I've got to concentrate.' Consequently, they are concentrating so hard on simply concentrating that they forget what they are on a golf course for — to hit the ball.

A method employed by many professionals in helping them concentrate is a planned routine in preparing to play their shots. One of Australia's favourite sons, David Graham, goes through such a routine.

Here's a six-point routine that can assist you with shot preparation and, subsequently, with concentration:

1 Line the ball up from behind and picture the shot you want to make.
2 Take your grip.
3 Address the ball with the clubface square to your intended line of flight.
4 Take up your stance, making sure your head is behind the ball.
5 Have a good look at the ball before commencing your backswing.
6 Begin your backswing with the thought of making a full extension and completing your shoulder turn.

The person who has a set routine in preparing for a shot has a far better chance of playing golf than the person who is too mechanical. Methodical preparation will keep you from being distracted by things that may be happening around you.

I would like to impress upon you
that if you choose to use the abovementioned
routine, or one similar, then don't waste time.
My six-point plan can be done quite
comfortably within 20 seconds. Time wasting
has become one of the biggest bugbears of
modern day golf and most of it occurs on the
tees and greens.

5

SET-UP JUST LIKE
CLOCKWORK

POSTURE in relation to set-up is most important for all golfers, but particularly for the beginner.

Take your stance about the width of your shoulders then squat as though you are about to sit on a chair at an angle of about 35 degrees with your weight evenly balanced. The hands should be positioned under your face, as you tilt forward. Just make half a backswing with a full follow-through, making contact with the ball using a downward movement. Let the loft of the clubface pick up the ball — that's what it's designed for.

Inconsistency in shotmaking is one of the biggest problems with beginners. They're forever trying to play perfect shots whereas the pros and outstanding amateurs make sure they don't play any bad shots. If you can get around the course making sure you don't play any bad shots, the end result will be most satisfying. And if you happen to play a great shot, that's a bonus.

Achieving consistency in your game comes from having a good grip, a good set-up parallel to the target and trying to swing every club at the same controlled pace. Correct set-up gives you a better chance of keeping the

CLOCKFACE METHOD

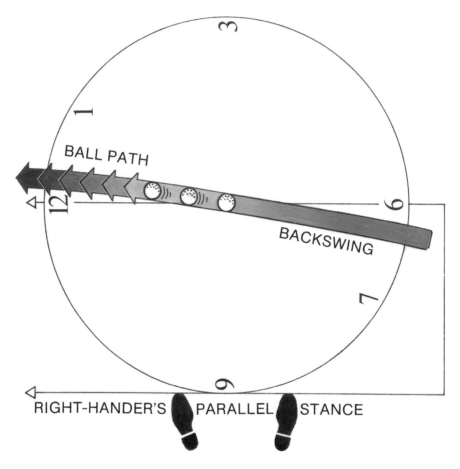

The clockface method of hitting: Take the club back between 6 and 7 then feel as though you are going to hit the ball between 12 and 1 with your wrists pronating through the impact area to impart draw on the shot.

CLOSED STANCE

Right foot drawn back slightly

OPEN STANCE

Left foot drawn back slightly

BEGINNER'S BALL POSITIONING

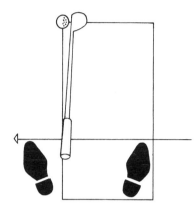

● WOODS AND LONG IRONS

BALL: Just inside left heel.
HANDS: Above or a little ahead of ball.
STANCE: Shoulder width.
WEIGHT: Slightly forward.

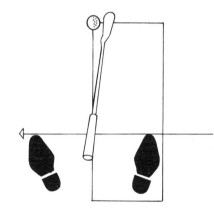

● MID-IRONS

BALL: Centrally positioned.
HANDS: Ahead of ball.
STANCE: Shoulder width.
WEIGHT: Favouring left side.

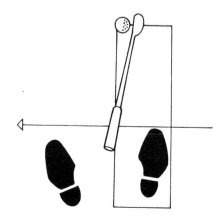

● SHORT IRONS

BALL: Slightly back from centre.
HANDS: Ahead of ball.
STANCE: Slightly open and narrow.
WEIGHT: A little forward.

ball in play than by being too closed or too open at address.

The clockface method will help produce a consistent swing. Picture a clockface on the ground with the 12 pointing in the direction of your target. The ball is in the middle and you are standing at 9 o'clock. Swing back between 6 and 7 to the top of the swing and when coming back through the impact area feel as though you are going to hit the ball between 12 and 1 o'clock, pronating your wrists through the impact area to introduce a little draw onto the ball.

ALL SQUARE AT ADDRESS

RIGHT: When taking your address, position the ball just inside the front heel (woods and long irons) with the hands slightly ahead of the ball and the front shoulder will be higher than the other, obviously due to the positioning of the hands. The head is slightly behind the ball, where it should be with all shots.

I recommend a stance about the width of your shoulders, depending on posture. If you are tall you may prefer a narrow stance, if you are short it could be wider. Whatever the case, your feet should be parallel to the line of flight and your weight fairly evenly distributed or slightly forward.

a) Place the front foot on an angle of about 40 degrees and the back foot can be square or slightly turned out, whichever is the more comfortable to allow you to pivot on your back ankle so that your leg doesn't collapse or lock on the backswing.

b) Get your back leg in a strong position to facilitate correct pivoting and coiling on the ankle throughout the backswing.

c) Bend your knees slightly as though you are about to sit on a chair with your bottom stuck out and your stomach tucked in.

d) Let the arms hang naturally under the face allowing freedom for a full swing. The dimples of the elbows (not the points) should point outwards. Don't lock your elbows into the rib cage ... that creates too much tension. As you hold the club, the shaft should be at an angle of about 45 degrees to the ground. The front arm should be a little forward of the back arm on your parallel line.

e) Have your head in a naturally relaxed position so that you can see the back of the ball.

COLLISION COURSE WITH TROUBLE

This open address is a common fault with many players where the back part of the body is too far forward of the rest, putting the player on a collision course with trouble. The open shoulders prevent a correct pivot or turn on the backswing and lead to shots being blocked out with resultant slicing of the ball or even dragging away with a square clubface.

HOOKING CAN BECOME A DRAG

Here the body is too closed where the player lines up too far right of the target to allow for a hook or drag. Invariably, in trying to correct this fault, the player closes his or her stance more and more and the problem then becomes compounded.

Roll your wrists through the impact area in the same manner as a tennis player does when hitting a topspin forehead shot.

6
DEVELOP YOUR OWN SWING

No two golf swing are the same.

I explain to my students that as long as they live they will never be able to swing a club like Greg Norman or Seve Ballesteros, Ben Hogan or Jack Nicklaus, Jan Stephenson or Pat Bradley. I look at the physical build of a person then design a swing to suit.

Work on a swing that's going to suit you, then your intention is on hitting the ball. Always use the same swing for every club in the bag, even though there is a sweeping movement for woods and a downward motion for irons.

Half a backswing is going to help while learning to play. It prevents overswinging and hitting from the top. You create bat-and-ball sense much quicker with a half swing, but always make sure you have a full follow-through.

One of the biggest swing faults with learners is they have a tendency to close the clubface on the backswing; that is, turning the clubface towards the ground. Just let the clubface fan with the toe pointing to the sky when half-way back, or pointing your thumbs to the sky, if you like. Don't try to keep the clubface square to the ball throughout the backswing. Let it fan a little and bring it back square to the ball at impact by pronating the hands. Pronating, in golfing terms, is to roll or rotate the hands or wrists through the shot. Many beginners get it in their minds that they must keep everything square throughout the swing. That's because they find it difficult to get over the feeling of trying to lift the ball off the ground or scoop it, instead of hitting it. Work a golf club as you would a tennis racquet or even a fly swat.

A narrow stance can also be a productive learning method, providing a feeling of hitting the ball at the bottom of the swing.

HEAD ALWAYS BEHIND THE BALL

ADDRESS: An ideal ball position is just inside the front heel. Hands are ahead of the ball and the front shoulder is higher than the back shoulder. Note that the head is behind the ball, where it should be with all shots.

PUTTING YOU IN THE DRIVER'S SEAT

MAKE A ONE-PIECE MOVEMENT

TAKEAWAY: Hands and arms to go back in a one-piece movement with the front ankle relaxing as the knee begins to shift towards centre. As the shoulders turn they automatically rotate the hips to the degree that is necessary to complete a full shoulder turn. Note that the toe of the club is pointing to the sky.

59

LEFT KNEE COMES BACK PAST BALL AS WEIGHT TRANSFERS

BACKSWING: The front ankle relaxes and the left knee comes back past the ball as weight shifts to the back side. Pivot on the back ankle, keeping the leg in a kink position and you're ready to drive through the ball. Make a 90 degree shoulder turn under the nose (not under the chin — see Chapter 8) and the clubface is at a 45 degree angle to the sky with a straight left wrist. Push your hands out (not straight up) to the sky, which aids in maintaining a consistently compact swing.

60

THIS IS WHERE YOU RIP INTO IT WITH YOUR RIGHT SIDE

DOWNSWING: The wrists are starting to uncock, weight is transferring off the back leg onto the front side which is starting to clear. From here you drive through the shot with the back hip and bottom hand, getting the back heel off the ground early (not quickly) to allow the knee to play its part in the driving action. The leading arm is firm and the back elbow tucks into the body. Again note, my head is still behind the ball.

61

FULLY EXTEND BOTH ARMS TOWARDS THE TARGET

EXTENSION: Try to make a long extension and keep the ball on the clubhead as long as possible. The longer you can keep the clubhead on the ball, the more control you will have over it and, therefore, the better chance you will have of keeping it on line. Extend both arms towards the target, pronating (rolling) your wrists, as though you would play a right-handed topspin tennis shot down the line ... for a winner. The back knee and ankle are relaxing as the weight transfers to the front side and the head remains in its position behind the ball before it was struck.

COMPLETE THE SHOT WITH A FULL TURN

FOLLOW-THROUGH: Apart from playing the game, the great thing about golf is the exercise you get. Here, the torso and head have turned completely towards the target with the weight now on the left side while balancing on the right toe. The further you follow through the better chance you have of getting extra distance.

HIT DOWN INTO BACK OF BALL WITH YOUR FAIRWAY WOODS

There is very little difference between the set-up and swing action of the fairway wood and the driver. Players who have difficulty in hitting fairway woods are generally those who try to lift the ball off the ground. What you should do is hit down into the back of the ball and allow the loft of the clubface to do the work in getting it airborne. Just try to hit the ball at the horizon. The fairway wood is the most beautiful shot in your bag of clubs.

7
FAN CLUBHEAD ON THE BACKSWING

T HE backswing begins by taking the club away with the arms and hands in a one-piece movement, keeping the clubhead square and low to the ground for the first 60 cm or 2 ft. From that point just let the clubhead fan gradually till you are halfway back, when the toe of the clubhead should be pointing to the sky with your weight transferring onto the back leg. The hands and arms are nearly halfway back before the body begins to coil, then continue on that arc with the shoulders turning to the top of the swing.

With the knees kinked, you are wound up over the top of your back foot. There isn't any sway even though you may feel as though you have moved about 30 cm or 1 ft. Don't overswing or collapse your knees out and away from your body.

Overswinging is a great problem with inexperienced players. They tend to break their wrists too early then take their hands to the top of the backswing without any body turn.

I recall, back in 1967, when my wife, Margaret, came to me saying: 'I can't hit this darn golf ball; I just can't get any distance. I keep flipping it up in the air and duffing shots.'

Upon inspecting her swing, I immediately noticed she was too wristy in her takeaway. She kept breaking her wrists too early. She wasn't getting any body turn because she was

When making your backswing, fan the club so that when it is halfway back the toe of the clubhead points to the sky.

picking the club up too soon on the backswing. This was causing her to overswing with the result that she was hitting the ball too early and the product of that is duffing, skinny shots and topping.

After correcting the fault and spending some time practising the one-piece takeaway, Margaret's game improved dramatically, so much so that in that same year she claimed the prized Gertrude McLeod Trophy for having reduced her handicap more than any other lady golfer in Queensland.

In the space of nine months her handicap plummeted from 35 to 19, a 16-stroke reduction — simply amazing, if I say so myself.

It is essential that the left side (for the right-hander) of your body remains as straight as possible once you have reached the top of your backswing. Don't tilt from the hips. That only negates the important function of body coiling throughout the backswing.

Beginning your downswing, feel your weight transferring onto the front side, with your hands pronating and releasing through the shot. Always keep your head behind the ball coming into the shot. You start the backswing with your head behind the ball, so keep it there throughout the swing.

In all bat-and-ball games, you must stay behind the ball to correctly execute a shot.

MID-IRON PLAY

LEFT AND BELOW: Position the ball just forward of centre in your stance and swing the same as you would with a fairway wood. Again, make a 90 degree shoulder turn; pivot on the back ankle and let the front knee go back past the ball.

BELOW: Make a good extension through the shot, the same as with woods, transfer your weight to the front side and keep your head behind the ball.

8
TURN UNDER
THE NOSE

T HERE has been a long-held misconception that the shoulder turn should be made under the chin, literally, i.e. across the throat.

Make your shoulder turn across your chin and under your nose. Turning under the chin can force the head out of position.

Many players misinterpret what the term 'under the chin' means.

If the front shoulder turns directly under the chin, it will force the head up and away from its naturally set position into a stretched position. This will cause a lifting feeling on the backswing and mishits then occur.

In order that your head remains in its natural position throughout the swing, turn your front shoulder under your nose. Yes, under your nose.

In other words, to complete a 90 degree turn, the shoulders will turn across your mouth or the point of the chin.

Of course, if you are one of those people with an extremely long neck then your shoulder turn is likely to be under your chin.

9

WRIST ACTION LIKE SWATTING A FLY

COMING back into the hitting area on the downswing, you should return the clubface square to the ball with a positive turn of the wrists. It's called releasing and is like a flick of the wrists at the bottom of the swing, from the back knee to the front knee. It can be likened to swatting a fly, or hammering a nail, or playing a topspin tennis shot. A positive turn of the wrists will eliminate slicing. You may feel as though you are going to hit the ball away from you slightly but, hit correctly, the ball will gradually draw back onto the target line.

I can remember when one of my former trainees, Paul Foley, kept slicing and fading the ball because he broke his wrists too early on the backswing. It was the cause of much frustration, for both him and me. So, one afternoon in 1978 I took Paul out for a round at Royal Queensland with the sole purpose of solving this 'affliction'. He had never been able to draw the ball before — bring it back from right to left for a right-hander. I had purposefully put six brand new golf balls in my bag and when we reached the par five third

One of my oustanding trainees, Paul Foley... a frustrated slicer who lost many balls before learning the correct wrist action to effect a draw.

tee, I knew this was the place to sort him out.
A ball hit to the right of this fairway is 'history'.
It is bounded by a huge drain and beyond that
is thick mulga (bushes).

Paul teed off and his drive cut out over the
drain into the mulga. He hit another and it
met with the same dreadful fate. Then I pulled
out one of those new balls and gave it to him,
saying: 'Righto, aim at that drain and bring it
back to the middle of the fairway.'

Straight over the drain it went again.

So I unwrapped another new ball, gave it to
him and said: 'Now, hit it at the drain again; hit
it away from you and make sure you release.
Take the club back in a one-piece movement
and don't let your wrists cock until you get to
the top of your swing.'

Into the 'drink' the ball went, so out came
another ball — No. 3. I gave him the same
instruction — aim at the drain. But, no, he still
sent it on a course of disaster.

Ball No. 4 emerged. Paul was so nervous
about the prospect of losing another of my
new golf balls that he said: 'I'd better make
this one release.' And he did. He hooked it
back onto the middle of the fairway. I gave him
a fifth new ball and said: 'Do it again.' He did.

From that day his slicing problem was
solved and he went on to win several
tournaments and become a recognised
Australian player.

Let it rip from the back knee and make a full extension.

10
BIG FOLLOW-THROUGH ADDS METRES

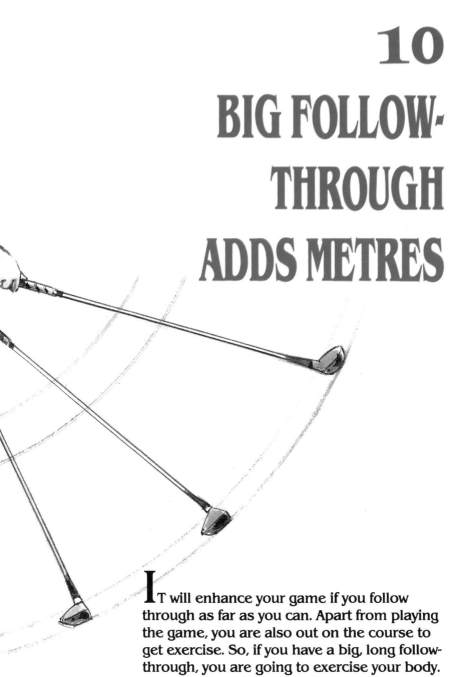

IT will enhance your game if you follow through as far as you can. Apart from playing the game, you are also out on the course to get exercise. So, if you have a big, long follow-through, you are going to exercise your body.

A way of making sure you follow through correctly is to use the clockface method (described in Chapter 5). Hit the ball between 12 and 1 o'clock.

If that doesn't suit, here are some other methods: Feel as though you are going to drag your leading arm back into the hitting area with the hands pronating for a full release from the back knee to the front knee; or transfer your weight earlier, always keeping your head behind the ball; or point the end of the grip at the ball through the downswing so that you keep your wrists cocked from the top of the swing back into the hitting area; or get the weight off your back foot early with the heel coming off and the weight shifting onto the inside ball of the foot in one of the first movements of the downswing.

The reason players come off shots is because they are unconsciously trying to hit up on the ball in their endeavours to get it airborne. This can be overcome with a correct follow-through.

And if you uncock your wrists too soon (at the top of the swing) you'll 'hit' the ball halfway down the downswing. Let it rip (release) from about the back knee. That is, uncock your wrists on the downswing from the back knee once the weight has gone through. You'll be amazed at what distance you can achieve.

11

THE WAGGLE BEATS COLD STARTS

T HE waggle, contrary to what some so-called pundits of the game may tell you, has a very important function in swing preparation. It serves as a starter, a trigger if you like, to a smooth backswing because, by waggling, you are relaxing your muscles to avoid a stiff takeaway. Having a waggle has definite advantages over beginning your backswing from a cold start.

The waggle also affords you the opportunity of making last-minute adjustments, whether it be to your grip, your feet or your alignment. You can't do this effectively if you stand frozen over the ball just before starting your backswing. The waggle provides physical and mental preparation to the swing and should be viewed as a vital part of your golfing armoury.

Don't be misled into thinking that the waggle is a useless mannerism. Many a great player has a waggle, and he or she uses it for the purposes I have explained — part of their preliminary routine to triggering their backswing.

The waggle serves a very useful purpose in triggering the backswing.

There are other forms of triggers to get your backswing in motion: a forward press with the hands; a turn of the hips; a tilt of the head; pressing your weight onto the front foot, etc.

Gary Player uses a back knee press to set his backswing in motion. Jack Nicklaus turns his head to the right before beginning his takeaway. This is a very good movement because his chin is already clear of his left shoulder when he completes his shoulder turn.

For those now wishing to develop a waggle or trigger action, don't let it get out of hand to the point where it becomes an uncontrollable addiction. I've seen this happen to even some world-class players.

Swing at a pace that will give you warning signs on your backswing of anything going wrong. Always keep your swing under control to develop consistency.

12

CONSISTENCY COMES FROM A CONTROLLED SWING PACE

GOLFERS need to find a swing pace or rhythm that will suit them. Some are quick in their actions; some are slow. Look for a pace that is going to let you feel the clubhead coming into the hitting area square to the ball and consequently square to your target.

You should swing at a pace that is going to give you warning signs about anything going wrong on your backswing — cocking your wrists too early; picking the club up too quickly, etc. When you swing too quickly you don't feel those things. Conversely, swinging too slowly will result in loss of rhythm. If you can swing every club in your bag at the same controlled pace, you have a chance of being consistent and, thus, eliminating trouble. It is a game of co-ordination and timing.

And as many of us know, there are several things which can affect our co-ordination and timing — anxiety, nerves, rushes of blood, etc. It is difficult to overcome. You simply have to practise at attaining a consistent pace and take it into competition with you.

FAILING TO RELEASE

Having been told that hands must be ahead of the ball on all shots, many players exaggerate the position to the point where they fail to release on their shots. The end result is too much movement past the ball, blocked shots, duffed ones or topping.

SCOOPING SKYWARDS

This is a scooping action, the result of not transferring weight correctly by staying too far back on the back foot. This ball will fly high.

A 'PHONEY' EXTENSION

This is like swinging inside a telephone booth — too narrow a swing with very little extension. It comes from staying on the back foot too long by not transferring weight. It's a Sunday arvo mixed fourball swing!

13

THE ART OF DRAWING AND FADING

OUTSTANDING golfers play with a draw or fade and if they just happen to hit the ball straight they are not in any real trouble.

When you try to play straight, quite often you don't know if the ball will go left or right.

The majority of good golfers prefer to play with a draw as it gives a little more distance. On the other hand, if you are a strong, long hitter, you might want to develop a fade into your shots. The fade is an advantage when attacking greens because it helps the ball land softer with less run.

Then again, a lot of the world's great golfers play with draw — Nicklaus, Player, Norman, Ballesteros, Crampton and Thomson. However, they are also able to play each hole as it comes, fading a shot whenever necessary.

To set up for a draw:
a) Aiming a little right of your target, address the ball with a slightly closed stance which will allow you to take the club away on an inside plane and thus hit the ball away from you.

b) Turn your front shoulder (which is higher than the other) a little towards the ball at address. This will help you pivot better and keep your head behind the ball.
c) Release into the shot, rolling your wrists and keeping your head behind the ball while allowing your hips to go past the ball first.

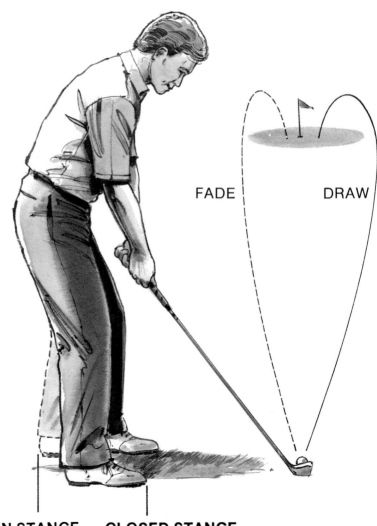

FADE   DRAW

OPEN STANCE   **CLOSED STANCE**
TO EFFECT FADE   **FOR DRAW SHOTS**

d) Clear your hips on the follow-through, making sure you complete your turn.

To set up for a fade:
a) Address the ball with the stance and shoulders slightly open to the target and the clubface aiming at your target.
b) Swing parallel to your feet and shoulder alignment which produces a swing plane that is a little outside the target line.
c) Stay outside on your downswing, coming across the ball slightly with your hands in front of the ball.

Correct set-up is the key to keeping the ball in play. If you want to play to the left side of the fairway, hit from the right side of the tee. The reverse situation applies to hit to the right of the fairway. This 'opposite' method gives you more fairway to work with. Pick out a reference point in the distance to shoot at.

When drawing or fading shots, there isn't a great deal of variation in your set-up.

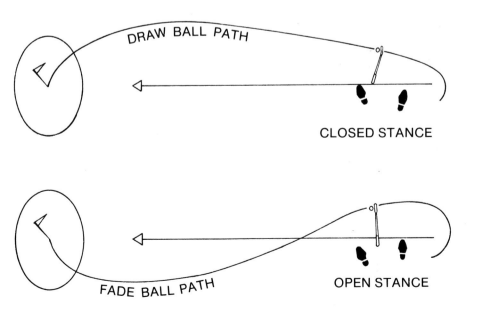

DRAW BALL PATH

CLOSED STANCE

FADE BALL PATH

OPEN STANCE

UPHILL SHOTS

LEFT: Standing below the ball, play it further back in your stance than normal and target yourself to the right as the ball will hook. The ball flies high from these lies so it wouldn't do any harm to take one club more and hit with a slightly open clubface. Even though you may feel as though you are leaning back, your hands still must be ahead of the ball.

RIGHT: With your feet above the ball, you will still get a hook shot from this uphill lie so again aim right. Take a wide stance for balance with your weight to the back and play the ball from a forward position with the clubface a little open. Set your hands ahead of the ball and your head behind it. Again the ball will fly high so select a longer club. As there are several aspects of this stance which are unorthodox, your swing will be restricted to a three-quarter arc.

SIDEHILL SQUATS

When standing above the ball it is important to squat to bring your arc down to the ball ... and stay on that level throughout the swing. Because of the difficulty with the stance, maintaining balance is all important and a full swing and follow-through are out of the question. You will need a club or two longer to make allowances for the restricted swing and also the fact that the ball will fade from such a lie. Take a slightly open stance and hit the ball a little further back than normal.

CAUTION DOWNHILL

Balance again is a vital factor for this testing shot. A point to keep in mind when not hitting from level ground is to position your weight on the contour of the land. In this case your weight is forward and the ball is played back a little from a slightly open and wide stance. To maintain balance, don't make a full-blooded swing and, as the ball will fly at a lower trajectory than normal, one club less should suffice. A slice is on the cards here, so aim left. Note that the head is behind the ball and hands are forward.

Peter Senior: he hit 6000 practice balls to learn how to use his trigger finger after I adjusted his faulty grip (see p. 29). Photo: courtesy of the *Queensland Golfer.*

14

WILL PUTTS INTO THE HOLE

THE basic ingredient to becoming a good putter is to get your eyes over the ball to create an L shape from the eyes, to the ball, to the feet. The grip should be one that suits the individual, but never too tight.

Putting is a one-piece action, keeping the wrists firm and creating a pendulum swing with the arms.

One of the major faults, especially on short putts, is allowing the front shoulder to move forward laterally when making the stroke. This is mainly caused through anxiety. Once the front shoulder is set, whether you have an open or closed stance, it stays put.

You should also set yourself up with your weight slightly forward, hands a little ahead of the ball and your head just behind the ball.

I would recommend standing slightly open when putting, to get a better look at the line. It's like throwing a ball underarm. This works for chipping and bunker play as well. It gives the feeling of standing behind and in line with the target.

Standing square while putting could give some players a crowded feeling. However, there are those who stand square and those

Get your eyes over the ball to form an L from eyes to ball to feet.

who are closed and they are good putters. If you are a good putter, don't change your style.

The more confidence you have putting, the more putts you are going to sink. Try to will the ball into the hole. You'd be surprised how many go in. Confidence in putting comes from having a sound stroke and the ability to read the line to the hole.

If you are not happy with your stroke — maybe you are pushing or pulling those vital short putts — open your hands a little. This will relieve tension and assist in keeping the blade square.

There are several suggested ways in which to see a line to the hole, but one that I recommend is to envisage a channel to the hole. When you set yourself up for a putt, try to visualise a channel, about the width of your putter head, running to the hole. The logic of this is that it is much easier to keep the ball within a channel than it is to stay on a single line. There is no point in letting the ball walk a tightrope.

The advantages of sinking putts lie in the imagination, so it is a definite advantage to think big once you have reached a green. It will enhance your ability to sink putts if you can see the hole larger than life. A way of doing this is to look at the back of the cup when sizing up a putt. This will help you to absorb the entire circumference of the hole. Putting to the back of the cup has the added benefit of giving you an attacking stroke. It stands to reason that if you putt to the back of the hole you won't leave too many short.

Those who putt to the front of the hole quite often experience the frustrations of leaving crucial putts short. These players don't have an appreciation of the entire hole.

Consider the comparison of trying to throw a cherry into a cup from a range of about 2 ft (60 cm). Shooting for the back of the cup

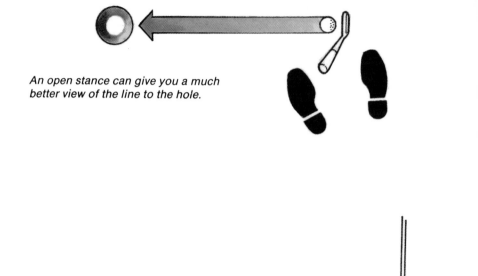

*An open stance can give you a much
better view of the line to the hole.*

*Putting to the back of the hole lets you absorb the entire circumference
as well as giving you an attacking stroke.*

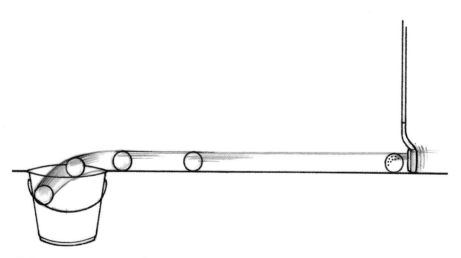

Think big when you walk onto a green. See the hole as big as a bucket.

certainly narrows the margin of error more so than trying to lob the cherry in just over the front lip.

SHORT PUTTS

The closer you get to the hole the more careful you need to be, and that particularly applies to short putts. Your body must remain still when handling these tiddlers; putt the ball at the back of the hole; and don't make any lateral movement on the stroke. If nerves begin to affect your stroke, open your hands slightly to relieve tension.

Don't spend too much time working out ways to miss short putts. One of the classic quotes about putting, which has always stuck in my mind, was made by one of this country's greatest golfers, Ossie Pickworth: 'If you are going to miss 'em, miss 'em quick.'

LONG PUTTS

If you picture the hole enlarged to about 2 ft (60 cm) in diameter you will increase your chances of getting the ball close rather than just putting at the object as it sits in the ground, a mere 4¼ in (108 mm) in diameter. Remember what I said earlier about imagination.

The best method for long putting was taught to me by a Scotsman, Archie MacArthur, about 25 years ago when he was the club professional at Gailes, near Brisbane. He told me to get my practice bag, which contained about 100 balls, stand about 100 ft (30 m) from a hole and putt all those balls at that hole.

Archie said to me: 'It doesn't matter if they go too far past or finish well short, as long as you can get the ball on line. You can judge your pace later.'

So I did this many, many times until I acquired a 'feel' for long putts. I also visualised a channel running to the hole when I practised, even from 100 ft (30 m) out. I teach the channel method for putting and for chipping.

Whatever theories you are taught or methods you employ, it all comes back to confidence. Never entertain negative thoughts. Always think that every time you hit a shot, whether it be a putt, a chip or from out of a bunker, it is going to go in the hole.

Adopt a positive approach with your short game and you'll be in for some pleasant surprises.

UNDULATIONS

There is little I can suggest to you on how to read slopes on greens other than to say that it is a matter for your own judgement.

When the ball is going to take fall (curve on its path) several factors must come into consideration, especially the speed of the green and the pace of the putt. If you are going to attack the putt then, naturally, the degree of fall will be reduced. Here, again, it all comes back to 'feel' and having a positive attitude.

No matter which way the putt is going to turn, still look for that channel to the hole I talked about earlier in this chapter.

SPEED

When you walk onto a green, take the opportunity to feel if it is hard or soft underfoot and observe the texture of the grass. If the green is hard or the grass is cut short or appears shiny, you will be faced with fast putts.

Greens tend to look shiny towards the end of a day's competition after dozens of shoes have trampled the grass down, particularly around the cup. You often see tournament players making close inspection of the texture

*The toe putt will produce
a slower ball speed on fast
greens.*

of grass around the hole. They do this to determine green speed.

Fast greens call for much caution with the putter, particularly those tricky downhill ones. If you want to produce a 'slow' putt from your normal stroke, simply hit the ball on the toe of the blade and it won't run as much as usual. The toe stroke deadens the blow.

If the putting surface is well grassed and has nap, it will be a slow green and a firmer stroke than normal will be required. You can produce more run on the ball by keeping the blade close to the ground throughout your stroke.

Another factor which can affect a putt's pace is grass grain. If the ball runs against the grain it will travel more slowly than it would with the grain.

Don't let the ball walk a tightrope. Look for a channel to the hole and putt within it.

The reverse overlap grip.

PUTTING GRIPS

The overlap or Vardon grip.

A popular grip where the index finger of the top (left) hand is placed over the fingers of the bottom hand. This helps in keeping the hands working as a team.

Setting up for a putt I recommend using a slightly open stance which will give you a better look at the line to the hole as your body will be behind the ball. It's like throwing or bowling a ball underarm. Have your eyes over the ball so that you form an L shape with the line from your eyes to the ball to the hole and another L shape with the eyes-ball-feet line. Don't grip too tightly, putt with a pendulum action with your arms and keep the top wrist firm. There is no body movement. Generally, the ball is positioned just forward of centre.

This is an example of a common fault with putting. The front shoulder has pulled away, bringing the torso around towards the target which results in dragging or pushing of putts. Don't make any lateral movement on putts. The shoulders must remain horizontal in order that you can stroke the ball along the intended line.

CHIP AND RUN IS JUST LIKE PUTTING

Here we have one of the best stroke-saving shots in the book. Played from just off the green with no hazards to negotiate, there is nothing complicated about the chip and run, which means exactly that: Chip the ball onto the putting surface and let it run up to the hole. Just stick to the basics. Take a narrow and slightly open stance with your weight a little on the front foot. The ball is positioned about the middle of your stance with your hands set slightly ahead of the ball. Grip the club short. Play the shot with your arms and hands with little cocking of the wrists and almost no body movement. It is similar to the putting stroke. In fact, it may help to imagine you are making a long putt and you may even choose to use a putting grip, which lessens hand tension. Select a club that will keep the ball at a low trajectory. The least lofted clubs are preferred, but the object of this shot is to make sure the ball lands on the putting surface. If the frog-hair is good enough to putt over, the Texas Wedge might be a better club choice.

15
SWING STAYS THE SAME IN FAIRWAY BUNKERS

T HERE are no special tricks involved in extricating a ball from a fairway bunker and sending it a fair distance. Obviously, it is essential that you hit the ball first, but there is no need to change your swing action.

If the ball is lying well, select a club that is going to give you ample clearance over the bunker's lip. If it is a shallow trap, you could go at it with a long iron or wood; if there is a steep bank to clear, obviously you will need a more lofted club.

Whatever your choice, address the ball with a slightly open stance and also open the face of the club a little to effect better elevation. Position the ball more forward than normal in your stance, further forward if you want more loft.

It is not advisable to take a full-blooded swing in a fairway bunker. Three-quarter pace will suffice and if you are in range to hit the green, use one or two clubs more.

You can ascertain the texture of sand when you walk into a bunker by looking at your footprints. Obviously, if it is dry the sand will be floury and care will need to be taken in ensuring you make solid contact with the ball. Sand compacts when wet and the surface becomes hard, allowing the ball to sit up much better than it would on soft sand.

And for those who don't know, you are not allowed, under the rules of golf, to ground your club in a sand bunker.

NORMAL WEDGE CHIP

The clubface is slightly open as is the stance and the ball is positioned inside the front heel with your weight forward. Don't hurry the backswing and hit the ball with a crisp, chipping stroke and an abbreviated follow-through. There is almost no body movement.

WEDGE SQUEEZE CHIP

If you have a fair amount of fringe to chip over and you want to stop the ball quickly, this is the shot that will do it. With an open stance, play the ball off the inside of the back heel with hands well ahead while using a short grip. Your knees are pressed towards the target and the weight is on the front leg where it remains throughout the shot. Close the clubface slightly and, with a punching swing action, send the ball in low, making sure it lands on the green. There will be plenty of backspin on this shot and the ball will check up quickly.

DON'T LET THE ROUGH BEAT YOU

Recovering from the rough is like playing a greenside bunker shot. You must pick the club up (reduce your extension) on the backswing, hit down sharply on the ball and make sure you follow through. The ball will 'pop' out of the long grass, similar to the way it explodes from sand. Because the clubhead has to work its way through long grass, this is a shot you have to hit hard with a firm grip, but not vice-like. Irons are preferred to woods and don't try to be greedy by going for distance. Your main objective is to get back into play and not to try to hit the ball onto the green. If you try to bite off more than you can chew, you could end up dropping more than one shot. I would suggest you try to extricate yourself from the rough with a fairly lofted club, playing the shot with a slightly open clubface, the ball in a forward position, weight on the front leg and hands set ahead of the ball. Give it all you've got, get back onto the fairway and, who knows, you may salvage par.

16

DON'T BE GREEDY IN THE ROUGH

YOUR main objective when playing from the short rough — which is prevalent throughout the world now — is to make sure you get back onto the fairway. Many players end up having two or three shots in the short rough because they try to play a normal stroke.

For best results: take an iron with suitable loft and open the face; pick the club up on the backswing similar to a bunker shot; hit down in a steep descending action, making sure you get the ball first; and make sure you follow through. The ball should fly out of the rough and you could pick up 60–70m, sometimes 100 m.

Don't be greedy. Make sure you are only going to drop one stroke instead of taking two or maybe three of these 'quail' shots where the ball runs across the ground and sits down again quickly. Open up the face ... chop ... it'll fly.

Irons are preferred to woods.

BUNKER PLAY NOT ALL THAT DIFFICULT

BELOW: Under normal conditions and with a reasonable lie, the greenside bunker shot isn't all that difficult. For the average player your objective is to get the ball on the green in one shot. Don't complicate matters by trying to be too cute. Work your shoes into the sand for a firm footing with a slightly open stance about the width of your shoulders. The clubface is open with your hands just ahead of the ball and your head behind the ball. Your weight is evenly balanced.

ABOVE: Pick the club up sharply with a lot of wrist cock and keep your head still behind the ball. Entering the hitting area, the wrists are still fully cocked, the clubface is still wide open and weight shifts to the front side.

DON'T TRY TO BE TOO CUTE IN THE SAND

RIGHT: Whipping your hands into the impact area, hit the sand about an inch and a half (4 centimetres) behind the ball. Look at the spot where you are going to hit the sand; don't look at the ball. Feel as though you are going to hit the sand with the back of the clubhead in a slapping action. This will allow the clubhead to skid under the ball. Don't hit the sand with the leading edge of the sand iron as it will dig in.

LEFT: It is most important that you follow through. A common error is trying to 'squirt' the ball out of the sand. It doesn't work. Don't quit on the bunker shot ... always follow through.
WET SAND: When sand becomes wet it compacts and you can't play a normal 'explosion'. Simply substitute your sand iron with a wedge or nine iron. With their less lofted faces, both these clubs have a better chance of taking more sand than the sand iron.

IT'S SOFTLY, SOFTLY ON BACKSWING

When playing the 'soft' shot sit well back on the heels with the left wrist straight and the clubface square. Take a long, slow backswing and extend through to the target.

17

CONFIDENCE CAN CURE THE YIPS

THERE are probably very few seasoned golfers who have escaped that dreaded 'disease' known as the yips. Even some of the best players in the world have been brought to their knees by the accursed yips.

I've gone through this problem. I get too much theory in my head of what I should and shouldn't do ... should I swing slower? ... are my hips turning too quickly? etc. I really do take my mind off the ball — and you can't do that.

People who suffer from the yips generally have their bottom hand taking control and it wants to push the shot through.

Those who claim they have a definite cure for the yips are having themselves on.

Probably the best way of tackling the problem — whether it be putting, chipping or bunker play — is to play with more confidence. I know it's easier said than done. Nevertheless, give it a try. What have you got to lose?

Try this: Imagine you are playing in a pressure situation when actually there isn't one. Keep working on this method and you could beat it.

It comes back to rhythm and pace so that you can 'feel' the clubhead through the shot and let it do its job.

If you have the yips with putting, open your hands to the point where your wrists can't break.

I reached the stage once where I couldn't even see the ball — it just disappeared. And Ben Hogan couldn't even get the putter back at one stage — that's why he gave up playing tournaments.

Defeating the sockets or shanks, you have to be very determined with yourself and say you are going to make the shot. Take a positive approach. It doesn't matter if you duff the shot, because you probably would have done that in the first place. So, be positive and play confidently and most times it will work.

Putting nerves can be reduced by opening your hands so that the wrists won't break during the stroke.

SIT BACK FOR LOFTED PITCH

Playing the lofted or soft pitch over a bunker or water hazard is a confidence shot. And achieving the desired result makes for one of the most satisfying shots in the game and certainly a stroke-saver. Sit back on your heels with your knees well flexed. Play the ball off the inside of the front heel with a wide open clubface. Your hands are ahead of the ball and hang under your chin. Open your stance and body towards the flagstick which will allow you to extend the club through to the target. Again, the club is gripped halfway down the rubber and your weight is prominently forward. Make sure your head is behind the ball at all times. See following pages.

115

USE A SMOOTH SWING AND POP THE BALL UP IN THE AIR

LEFT: With a firm action, make a smooth, unhurried backswing with a full cock of the wrists. Notice how the end of the club is pointing at the ball, an example of how far you need to take the club back.

RIGHT: Hit the ball with a firm, crisp action on an outside-in swing path that, associated with the open clubface, will pop it up in the air with plenty of backspin. The follow-through is abbreviated with the hips turning towards the hole and the head still behind the ball position. Finish off with all your weight on the front side, and the back leg relaxing with the heel lifting and the knee turning past the impact spot.

FIRM ARM NEEDED FOR HALF SHOTS AND PITCHING

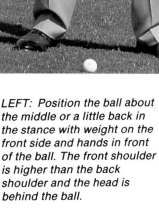

LEFT: Position the ball about the middle or a little back in the stance with weight on the front side and hands in front of the ball. The front shoulder is higher than the back shoulder and the head is behind the ball.

ABOVE: Note the strong front arm with little cocking of the wrists and only a minimal transference of weight.

EXTEND FULLY ON HALF SHOTS

When playing half shots, you must transfer your weight fully, as clearly demonstrated here. Make a full extension and a definite roll of the wrists.

119

That's me (the old bloke in the middle) with trainee professionals during an intensive training course at Brisbane's Victoria Park course this year.

Photo: courtesy of the Queensland Golfer

18
THE
PSYCHOLOGY
OF TEAMWORK

CLUB selection is most important when attacking the green, as is having confidence in your selection of club. You might need to run up with a seven or eight iron, or float a shot in, depending on the weather and playing conditions.

Picture the shot you are going to play. That's part of the mental approach to this game. And another mental method, one which I have employed from time to time, is to think of your clubs as 'Your Team'. No matter how many clubs you have in your bag, they are Your Team for the day.

A very important member of Your Team is the guy who has to hit the ball from the tee to get it into play so that all the other guys can do their job. The club you select to tee off with, whether it be a wood or an iron, you can call Mr Tee, and he has to get the ball into play.

Then, depending on your next shot, you have all those other guys to choose from and, whoever you select, it is his job to get the ball on the green (if it's a par four). If he doesn't, then you can call on Mr Wedge, or Mr Nine Iron or Mr Sandiron, who are good players around the green.

Once they have done their job, the main member of the team, Mr Putter, can finish it off and knock the ball in the hole. What about it, Team?

Sharing a light-hearted moment with a class of my more attractive pupils at Royal Queensland club. Photo: courtesy *The Courier-Mail*, Brisbane.

19

DON'T RUSH PRACTICE – IT'S A LEARNING PROCESS

IF there's one word I can impress upon you to help improve your golf — a word I emphasised at the beginning of this book — it is PRACTICE.

After I give my pupils their first lesson, I tell them that as long as their hands are not too sore, hit more golf balls. The more balls you hit at practice, the better you will become. And I'm not suggesting that you hit as many balls as you possibly can during a session. That would be a complete and utter waste of time.

Your practice plan should be to hit around 60 balls in an hour. You must be deliberate in your preparation for each shot and, after you have hit, carefully study the result. At the end, there are likely to be some questions you could ask your coach at the next lesson.

Start your practice session by checking your grip, then your swing. Just try some half swings to feel your weight is transferring correctly. Following that, go through your set-up procedure. Begin by hitting 10 to 20 half shots with a short iron to get your limbs operating smoothly and your muscles warmed up, then advance to longer shots. Line up your shots as you would if you were on a golf course, shooting to an imaginary flag.

Practice is to be treated as a learning process and is not to be rushed. What you are doing at practice is training your mind and your muscles to work as a team. Don't be like the players who are always running late for the tee and decide to have a quick warm-up before hitting off. They make a mad dash to the practice area with a bucket of balls, don't bother limbering up, immediately pull out a driver and go whack. Chances are they are going to do themselves an injury, like tearing a muscle, and then their day is destroyed, with golf being out of the question for at least a fortnight while they recuperate.

No, ladies and gentlemen, your practice time is not to be conducted at a speed that reminds one of a Keystone Cops movie. If you can't allow yourself enough time for a generous practice warm-up before hitting off, just do some easy limbering up exercises and be satisfied with that. Certainly, that's far better than risking injury.

For the player who is receiving tuition, practice between lessons will help your qualified PGA coach to help you. If you fail to practise between lessons it's like taking two steps forward and one step backward.

It would take an average of six lessons for a beginner to become reasonably competent to tackle nine holes or more — that is, of course, if he or she practises between each instruction.

20
HOGAN'S DETERMINATION AN INSPIRATION

WHEN I started playing golf in 1953 I went to see a movie called *Follow the Sun*, which was a portrayal of the life of the great American player, Ben Hogan. Glenn Ford played the role of Hogan and the film taught me a valuable lesson about determination.

I admired Hogan because he was a guy who had the guts to gnaw away and overcome obstacles which confronted him. He was a perfectionist. He worked hard at making his swing compact so that nothing would go wrong. He concentrated so hard when he was playing tournaments that he wouldn't talk to people. That's why he was so unpopular.

Nevertheless, his determination gave me the flair to keep trying; to keep gnawing away. This rubbed off on a lot of players he competed against throughout the world.

One of this country's great players, Norman von Nida, speaks highly of Hogan for his dedication to the game. And The Von was a very dedicated man himself. I can remember him hitting a poor three iron shot in a tournament. After the round, he went straight to the practice fairway and hit 300 to 400 balls with that three iron, just to get it right. Lee Trevino did the same thing with bunker shots. I also admired Sam Snead for the smoothness of his swing. It seemed effortless. It must have worried the hell out of some of his rivals.

Talking about smooth swings, I had the good fortune to be taught by a great swinger in Reg Want who, between the years of 1948 and 1952, was considered the best iron player in this country. I learned a lot from him, not only from what he taught me, but also from simply watching him play.

I gained a treasure of knowledge about the swing from watching the good golfers at practice and play. Every time I went away to tournaments I would go and look at the top boys in the bullring — I can still see Gary Player and Arnold Palmer. Australian greats, Kel Nagle and Peter Thomson, had uncomplicated swings. They didn't strive for distance; instead they sacrified length to keep the ball on the fairway... and it all came back to chipping and putting.

By watching the great swingers and hitters throughout the years, it has helped me with my teachings. I have used all their swings at sometime or another to get the message across. Even though Hogan was my idol, I haven't used his techniques specifically when giving instruction. The basics I teach are in the simplicity of the golf swing as used by Nagle and Snead and also players I have taught — namely Greg Norman, Corinne Dibnah, Ossie Moore and Mike Ferguson.

One thing this game, and life in general, has taught me is to listen to the voices of experience ... listen and learn, as the saying goes. Apart from instruction from my peers, I also gained much knowledge from listening to some talented amateurs.

The years have added a few extra inches to the waistline and quite a few grey hairs to the crown, but there's no doubting the physique and masterly style of the great Arnold Palmer. The year is 1963 and Palmer tees off on a par three at Royal Queensland in an exhibition match with (from left) Japan's leading tournament player of the day, Hideyo Sugimoto, the tall New Zealander Bob Charles — the only left hander to have won the British Open — and myself, small but tenacious. The caddies, who today hold club jobs, are Robbie Gibson (with Charles), Merv Ullman (obscured by Palmer) Barry Vassella (Earp) and John Dyer (black shirt, Sugimoto). I wasn't overawed by the illustrious company. I shot four under par on the homeward nine to square the match with my partner, Arnie.

Twenty-four years on from the 1963 exhibition. . . . what a fine body of men. We got together for a reunion photograph at the 1987 Seniors tournament at Tweed Heads, the club where I did my traineeship. From left: Robbie Gibson, Bob Charles, Merv Ullman, myself and Barry Vassella.